ROMANCE

ANN SANSOM

10 Nov. 94.

◉

Romance

for Janet

with love
+ thanks ———

I took note of your
suggestions – for what
my taking note is worth

A ×

BLOODAXE BOOKS

ISBN: 1 85224 285 X

First published 1994 by
Bloodaxe Books Ltd,
P.O. Box 1SN,
Newcastle upon Tyne NE99 1SN.

Bloodaxe Books Ltd acknowledges
the financial assistance of Northern Arts.

Cover printing by J. Thomson Colour Printers Ltd, Glasgow.

Printed in Great Britain by
Cromwell Press Ltd, Broughton Gifford, Melksham, Wiltshire.

ROMANCE:

'Your romance writers are likewise a set of men, whose authority I shall build upon very little.'
– ADDISON, 1713

'To compose in verse.'

'A tale written in the vernacular. Any fictitious or wonderful tale: a fictitious narrative in prose or verse which passes beyond the limits of real life.'

'Of a fabulous or fictitious character, having no foundation in fact.'

'Having no real existence; imaginary; purely ideal.'

'An inferior form of literature, chiefly for women.'

Acknowledgements

Acknowledgements are due to the editors of the following publications in which some of these poems first appeared: *The Guardian, London Magazine, The North, Poetry Review, Poetry with an Edge* (Bloodaxe Books, new edition 1993), *The Red Deer Anthology* (Red Deer, 1992), *The Rialto, Times Literary Supplement, The Virago Book of Wicked Verse* (1992), *The Wide Skirt* and *Writing Women.*

Other poems in this collection appeared (under the name Ann Dancy) in *Painting from Memory* (Smith/Doorstop, 1989), *Suitcase* (Blue Rose Books, 1989) and *Opening the Ice* (Smith/Doorstop Books, 1990).

Thanks are due to Yorkshire & Humberside Arts for a New Beginnings Writers' Award given in 1994.

Contents

Base Linguistics

A morning of received pronunciation:
subtle differences between the *ah* and *oh*
fricatives, bi-labials and a diagram
of how the teeth may work together with the tongue.

Midday we adjourn/retire/repair to the pub. Wordy
but if we speak now, if we ever open up again
it will be too much, too wide, too soon.

We are not girls. We weigh the things we're told
and there is little that we swallow whole
but sometimes there's a joke that makes you smile
in the dark. It may be weeks before it makes you sick.

Have you heard the one, he said, About the graduate
who couldn't count to twenty-eight? She had.
She's smart, she's numerate and anyone can calculate

four women divided by two elbows on a table divided by
an ashtray, a full round of dead glasses united by
five kids, a series of old debts, divided by one man
and multiplied again. Anyone. It's a simple equation.

But for all our command of semantics, lexis,
the clear physiology of speech, women fresh from lectures
women awash with nausea and beer are seldom articulate.

She slurs it. Alive to the fact that words
are often mouth and air and her answers lie
in neat subtraction, she states it. *He'll blame me.*
And she can place it. It dates back months,

it dates back years, it dates back to the apple.
Between us we have the plosives, the stops,
the hard core that sticks in the throat

and makes us dumb. Together we discover
that there are no synonyms, no common tongue
to cover every case and gender
but there is safety of a kind in numbers.

Cross Country

It was genuine – real fox –
when she knew no better
(traps and the contemplation of pain,
the rights of the living)
and she guarded and nursed
and hugged it to her
from Darlington to Doncaster,
crooning into the collar.

At York, in the five-minute break,
she ran through the sleet –
shouldering the coat, a big soft sleeping child,
the sleek inlay spotted
and starred with wet, the tie ribbons trailing –
and came back breathless, scenting
the compartment with musk and chocolate.

There was an oval compact,
steel and red enamel that she opened,
scowled into, and snapped shut, satisfied.
And he was talking, giving her
the benefit of his philosophy.
The secret of happiness.
Own nothing. Want nothing.

Backing in past St George's,
the snow circled, settling briefly
shifting on the dark; the lights
in the goods yard, the sidings,
slowing, *We are now approaching...*
And in the three minute tunnel
he told her, All journeys end.
And that is the beauty of them.

Does this coat have Buddha-Life?
Open it. Here in the hem,
eleven flat lead weights.
A master number. Count them.

There is suffering, my dear,
and there is non-attachment. Allow me.
Seven linings. Brown silk on grey silk
on unbleached linen. Reach past
these layers of nylon, hessian,
netting, the pulse in your fingertips.
Feel. The moist suede innard of the animal.

Dark Room

(for Anne)

We are winding negatives by sound and touch,
listening for the grate of torn film,
the easy pull of half connected spools.
My eyes dilate till they ache
but it is your hand on my arm
that guides the scissors through the dark.

The red bulb comes on, we agree
about expensive restaurants, cheap clubs,
but we are speaking softly, measuring
like alchemists, filtering a solution
that smells like vinegar and bleach
through a seal that will not let in light.

Hip to hip we stand, rocking dishes
chanting the seconds almost in time.
Above, someone slams a door, runs,
heels come knocking on the stairs.
Your grainy ghost is cursing
frayed close-ups, over-exposed and dull,

but here, each tide I tip
mascerates the coated card,
breaks the memory in silver strips,
unlocks your eyes, contours your mouth,
and loose between my thumbs
your proven face comes sliding up.

From the moment I picked up your book

From the moment I picked up your book, I was convulsed.
One day I intend to read it.
GROUCHO MARX

I know you. I recognise the stumbling sway,
the way that you choose me. The full length
of an empty carriage and you choose me.
And you choose wrong. I'm busy here,

a *Sunday Sport* left on the seat – AMAZING
STONE AGE WOMAN FOUND ALIVE IN CAVE,
ASTOUNDING SEXY FEATS OF NEW AGE MAN –
Persuasion still unopened on the table,

the Walkman sizzling between two stations.
I'm occupied, engaged, but you move in
and with one swipe, clear off the debris,
spread your big white man-size hanky.

A tablecloth? And you intend to dine, perhaps?
A candelabra from your pocket, a violin, a rose
offered between here and Leeds? How dare you
interrupt a woman with two hundred pages

left to read, a woman who if you weren't here
could lie back with her feet up on the seat.
All right. I've been on trains before.
I know some people can be rocked

beyond restraint, made bold in transit,
and some will offer up the underside
of what they do in dreams and some
can't wait to show the things they do,

or want to do at home. And some.
I wonder, vaguely, where I'm going now,
where you are coming from...
Don't be deceived. This is not fear.

I shake because I'm venomous.
I'm white with murderous disdain.
I am this wall, this luggage rack, this door.
I am not here. And you are not

my final fellow traveller.
You're almost out of sight, midway
between the table and the vacant seat
and I repress the reflex, the sharp instinct –

no lady ever kicks a kneeling man
nor dares offend a crawling one.
I focus on the book, concentrate,
her carriage and deportment were quiet...

You reappear, a flushed and happy conjuror,
presenting, just between us, first one naked foot
she had been forced into prudence in her youth,
and then, in time, the other

she learned romance as she grew older.
The soles are very clean, almost unused.
You're barefoot, harmless. Who could take offence?
I'm calm. You're simply ignorant of rules.

But pedicures are always serious;
you frown to get it right. Perfectionist.
When every toe-nail's sliced
you scoop the creamy crescent clippings,

reach up, release them from the hanky,
fluttering from the window, sparse confetti.
A neat man. Tidy. Every action slow.
Your smile. The way you roll your socks

to a soft fist, slide it in your pocket.
Your smile. Your finger on the blade,
the way that you retract it. Your smile.
I remain polite. When you stand up

I nod to your *goodnight*.
And when you've really gone
I close the book
on all the times I had the sense

to cut and run and froze instead,
but paid for it in buckets of cold sweat.
This is where I dip my finger in
and draw the real hard line. I'm giving up

my corner seat, my common courtesy
to men who groom themselves
with Stanley knives, to gentlemen
who will not let me read in peace on trains.

Belle

Overnight in the corner house,
up in the turret: your guest bed
heated by the pink electric blanket
I'd left behind on my last visit –
two weeks extended to six months,
a year, *just relax, you're welcome here.*

And at four – woken by the trees
ticking like taxis, the lads
who come at dawn to screech
their fathers' cars around the park –
I lit a candle and, unable to rest,
went down for tea, a cigarette

and passed you, out of step
against tradition on the stairs;
the black cat at your heels,
a book of herbs, a glass of gin and water
balanced in one hand, the small axe
head down in your dressing-gown pocket.

My dear, caster of good spells
over a transient half-moon estate,
I'm worried now about the night they came
with a brace and bit and took apart
your door, your locks, and cut
your phone line. I'm worried for them.

Party

Pearl's at the table, hefting a big knife,
giving the cucumber what-for, hammering
the handle straight down to the board, singing.
The kitchen's clean, every surface covered
with food, cans, bottles; every surface shines
and we are settled, domestic as cats.
Certainly the hottest day this year
but she keeps the multi-coloured jacket on,
rolls up her sleeves and cools herself on lager.

Knock it back. We're celebrating too soon.
These cans sound empty and, with hours to go,
we should be measuring the whisky.
I check the oven, slosh water round the sink,
worry about the garden, open cupboards
and shut them, forgetting. She fills a glass.
I shuffle an ash-tray of ring-pulls. I want
to sleep, to have another drink. I want to stop.
You can't have everything, she says, *Sup up*.

When I come back from the phone, she's dancing;
the radio's retuned, turned up. I'm moving
despite myself, despite the lack of space.
Cards waver as we pass. Love, more love,
jokes, All my love... Some fall. 'I'm 39,'
I say, trying it out. *Well done*, she says,
and holds me closer, patting my shoulder
like a mother. My face is hot, I'm wondering
about opening windows, about falling out.

Tell tale tit your tongue will split
but this is my friend. I'll tell half.
She lights a cigarette, squints
to place it in my mouth, picks up a glass,
closes my fingers on it. 'A man
That's all. I'll be all right.' *Strikes me*, she says,
It's going to your head. Just sober up.
It's not too late. He's irresistible
but so's a finger down the throat.

The Courtesy of Butchers

The lad scrubs the block, both hands to the brush,
his knuckles raw, his back a twig. Ill bred, poor stock;
my kids are better fed, red as me. It's in the blood.

Delivery? No problem, duck. I smile, he scowls –
Don't come it, son. I load his basket, watch him pedal off,
the apron tucked up in his lap.

Bacon whispers out in shiny quilted steps; I offer it
on greaseproof, my scoured palm. All right, my dear?
Politest man you'll ever meet, honest

as my own pork pies, open as a walk-in fridge.
Best British Rump; Boiled Ham; Mutton.
I think Cow's Arse; Dead Pig; Old Sheep, and don't let on.

You see the light, it's me in here at night,
the shutters down. You'd not believe...
I swill my arms under the cold tap, they gleam, alive.

See this topside, shoulder? Feel it. Prime.
I know jokes you'd never get – Don't go without
your dripping, pet. I have to laugh...

They lean on the glass, eyes down, judge the goods,
grateful for a kind word, a bit of bull. I don't carve,
I sculpt and hold it out: That do you, love?

My card's on the counter: *Here to Serve.*

The Sisters of Mercy
(for Eva)

We've earned it. We burned our mouths enough
when we were young; on our backs in her father's shop
sucking sherry straight from the tap.
Tonight we deserve something from the top shelf.
We'll have the spirit with the strongest scent.

Ice keeps surfacing in mine: 'You should have
left it neat.' It's her voice
the morning I threw up, *Didn't you know
enough to stop?* Her fingers pressed
transparent on the glass, as if they might

just snap the stem or turn two decades back,
rubbing in the cold sweat on my neck...
But she has him to consider now; his new car,
his wife, these shoes he likes, her small feet
on his shoulders, the velvet skirt, the stain

I'd call ice-cream if I had it cleaned.
She talks too loud. Abrasive. Coarse.
She stares the landlord out. Hard face.

Once it was fragile in our hands, a full cup
we had to sip and take care not to drop.
Something failed in me and I let go
of my own life, the choice. 'Nuns or whores,'
she says, 'And guilt. Bedded in like broken glass.'

And so we drink to Sister Kevin, Sister Francis
and ourselves. Sister Michael, Sister Joseph
and ourselves. Her man and mine. Ourselves.
There's nothing brittle in us now,
we're mellow as good whisky, old pain

that brings detachment, liberation.
We're at ease together, shameless, innocent
as sleepers who'll do anything, say anything.
At the station she says, 'Don't cry.
Your face looks bad enough.' and turns away

to judge the talent on the tip-up seats
as if she were sixteen and could have anyone.
I put her on the train, kiss her, trust her
to do it for us both. Monday morning, Sketchleys
with the velvet skirt. 'I'll tell you straight.
You just tell me can you get it out.'

You'll be fine

(for Stuart)

Take aspirin. Take plenty.
But you sigh, readjust your elbow,
rest your face on the teapot.
Yes. Heat. That really works.
Sometimes. There's no rush.
You have a whole morning
to nurse the headache, to decide.

When Alice arrives, you kiss her
and go out to patrol the garden;
your jeans ripped in the wrong place,
your baggy political t-shirt,
your familiar profile oddly cut
and recut by the sheets, the nappies.
I share the beer with her.

Three years, two kids and it's on.
A few friends told. No family. No flowers.
'You OK?' she shouts.
Thumbs up from you, who are, after all,
all right. Even sober. Even today.
And I notice you've recovered the shears
from the hedge and are about to tangle

with the clematis or Russian Vine
or whatever it is...*'What is that?'*
'That's him,' she says, 'Whittling over nothing.
Hardly a major operation, is it? Vasectomy.'
You look back. We raise our cans to you.

Game

We take the hill, coast down the dark side,
the city laid out for us, made small, bright
as a fairground. I daren't look,
trying to hold a finger on the map,
keep up my half of the conversation
and scan for the turn off.

The car's full of smoke and *Femme* and us.
I like this, she says, leaning across,
getting the volume wrong.
Tom Waits bawls, *What's the point...*
She quietens him. She's singing now.

We're off the roundabout she always misjudges –
'Circled it four times one night,' she says,
forgetting who held the door open that time,
who navigated, hanging out into the fog.
'Look.' Straight into her unblinking stare.

Her argument is circuitous, full of holes,
but the momentum of metaphor being
what it is, I freeze. Watch both hands open
on the wheel. This area is familiar –
she puts her foot down. We're late.

At speed all things disintegrate. When we come to:
'You smell gorgeous. What's that scent?' I'm ready
with the lie and the smile, and I remember
last night, walking with a friend –
his doubt. My certainty:
'Women have no concept of Fair Game.'

Belle's Drawer

I put the book down on her desk,
precisely in the fitting square of dust,
readjust her anglepoise, her sliding stacks
of notes, first drafts. The window's double-locked

against the fog, rattling ivy, dried-out branches
and the half moon patio she launched into
with a hammer *here endeth summer*.
Small birds gather to pick over

yellow shoots among the rubble.
Last year we had the ordered herbs
and random bluebells, toadstools,
a wilderness of grasses. *Have sense*

she said, *relax*. A safe house
in a ring of wicked witch's trees.
Searching for the one clock in the place
I find I'm rummaging her drawer for clues.

I turn loose brown and purple rolls of money,
a rigid coil of orange peel, a labelled remedy
Insomnia/Anxiety, a box of pins and staples,
a deck of mislaid postcards, stubbed candles,

a ripped envelope, my own scrawl on it
I've fed the cat and let her out
no one phoned
wake me when you get home

I close it gently, my right hand
to lift and ease the faulty runner
and my left, a tangle I can't quite shake off
of gritty pink and blue and pink elastic bands.

Princess

You came rocking back from the south,
hanging off the seat, trying
to be still, be good for mummy
who'd known just the man
to right your little error.

And you sang nursery rhymes all night
to your pretty rosebud wall
to your glass and china frogs
to the photos of yourself.
You sang until the words came wrong

and then you clenched your knees
and cried and promised never never.
She hushed you, showed you in her mirror
mirror that connects how this begins
with how it sometimes never ends.

She cleared the room, cradled you
until you woke, then brought red wine
to build you up and celebrate
a close scrape, a lucky break, and you,
Princess, as good as gold, as good as new.

Is This Business?

Is this one hell of a night for a girl to be out;
vulgar as a boozy duchess, loud kissy as sleet on slabs,
chatty as maiden's water in the gutter? You tell me.
Your game, your taste, your price. You name it.
I'll turn it over on my tongue, spit like a connoisseur

but you're welcome, welcome
now the rain's let up, left the pavement glamorous,
a film; neon off the jewellers frayed in it,
these shiny shoes, a backing track
              I pass the freezer shop, the bank,
and stop at *Next*. He's barred and lit. He's nice.
My type. One big hard man
and cool and smart and what a suit...

Take care. I always say it after.
Turns me over, men who never speak,
men who say, You too, lover.
I look at them gone out. I'm lucky.
I'm smart as stilettos...Something special, love?
Just ask. Come on, don't fret. I'm tender
like the bag held flat inside my coat.
You're warm. I'll breathe in your hands,
thaw my face. My feet are mottled red and numb.
I pass. And you're just browsing, are you?
Maybe? And you want history, do you?
Same as yours, sweetheart.

Got to my feet an unlicked colt, barefoot
as a baby, naive as a new wife,
anything you like. We'll spin a tale,
turn a trick, feed a line. Who's hooked?
Who reels it in? Take care, my love.
Come back again. You're the best. Best I ever.
You, love. You can. You can tell me.
I'm soft, clean as a vicar's hand,
dirty as you want. The truth?
You want the one about my kids,
my debts, my dad? Want one of your own?

Come on. I'm safe as a mother.
Open my coat and see. Patent, plastic, empty.
Come on my dear my love my pet,
is this business or what?

Bridget

Nodding to half questions, she takes this one face to face.
Yes
once it was all I had, I wore it all weathers, inside out.
Then no warning I was eighteen
and I stopped lining men's pockets, just like that.
The Arabs were coming in, the price of everything shot up,
no joke, and there I was, still trying to sleep
on the Circle Line, eating when I could, dodging the cold.
All right.
We've all passed a lot of water under that bridge since then.
So, tell me Soho's come up in the world. God's honour,
haven't we all. But some things you carry,
some you keep, just in case; some things are in you.
Times I think there's nothing half so warm.

Then, it was the Sixties, Love, Revolution. Remember?
Forget it, baby. We're all set and Lennon's lost the password.
Eighty million in the bank. Can you blame him.
But the Underground suited me, I always loved the dark.

Sometimes I wake, alone, up to the neck in it
but still on my feet and I say, No more. Enough.
And believe me, I burn. Yes. Me.
So, come clean. You want to know, just ask.
Would I lie? There's no trick, it's there all right.
You really want to see?

Tips

You draw a map for my son, a cross for Leeds.
What a boy, wish he were mine. Yes,
with half your style, class,
the plated pen sheathed in a diary,
pages flickering fine as onion skin,
cigarettes with a gold band,
your narrow hand stubbing them
with half the life left in,
your lighter thin as an envelope.
There was a time, remember, I would
have picked your pocket for it.

Somewhere between us is a room
but this time furnished in good taste,
all yours. You turn the past
like a revolving door and I step in –
the waitress eases back into her shoe,
her apron corrugating, reaching for the bill.
My son flirts with her, you laugh aloud
and I can't drink any more.
You deal with the service charge.
I stand in the aisle and wonder,
do they still leave notes under the plates:
'your smile...your grace...'
then click their fingers, bring the wife to eat.

They make enough, you say in the street,
I don't leave tips for sluts.
The kiss for old time's sake
just misses.

Waterloo Road

The chaise longue wears a sheet for months
then we lever it into the skip, making space
for aircraft seats, a snip at five pounds a dozen.
The bed, another bargain, no mistake,
steel-framed, an ex-army mattress like an ironed wafer.
We pile pillows up to see the long run
of Waterloo Road, all those straight trees.
Like Paris, he tells me, only cheaper.

I want to read *Intimacy*. He interrupts:
Listen – flapping Genet's journals,
doing the Marlene Dietrich growl – listen.
Lend me the book, I think, but remember
last time. My mother was wild. *Our Lady
of the Flowers*. The sacrilege.
She wouldn't stop till the pages flew,
the cover reached the door ahead of me.
He's made a whore of you, shouted up the street.

Now I recognise my own cologne. He smiles.
Just a splash, to show you how you smell.
Yes. Like the Queen of Hearts t-shirt
for my birthday, bought in his own size.
You get five more minutes of this lamp.
'Even reading costs,' I mimic him.
'You're learning,' he says,
and takes my watch to mark his page.

Retreat

In a boxy convent bedroom, spilling it all –
Forgive me, Father. It is one hour
since my last confession. I forgot
the impure dancing/song/thought.

Excuse me, Father, but what is your position,
exactly, on mini-skirts/Mick Jagger/celibacy?
Strange, isn't it, Father, how silence
makes your mouth dry, how your lips seal

if you don't use them? You can tell me
anything, he said. It's what I'm for.
Examine your conscience and steady yourself.
What have you done so wicked, child?

Plimsolls gripping polished stairs,
one hand gripping the banister, I came down.
Soapy warmth from the kitchen, a line
of subdued girls, each waiting to be escorted up;

I let myself out. Who could tell me
anything? The world not open to question,
the world already full of spoiled priests
and a serious lack of men who listen.

Advance

Remember it like this.
You are on a platfrom, no longer believing
this is where you must catch your train.
A mistake. You'll admit it now.
The train will leave; the porters
are certainly discussing someone else.

You are in a buffet, swallowing something
you have no memory of having ordered.
You are looking down, intent on your glove.
You are exquisite, mannerly; your courtesy,
lack of appetite, astound you.
The word is tenderness. You are tender.

You will look at your ticket
and forget the destination a moment later.
The train gathers you. Towns trot like dogs,
sprint, fall back baying in tunnels.

You don't even glance. Nothing startles you.
Tell me, you say. And she does, quietly,
so you must lean forward. She receives it
like a hand cupped to her face;
eyes closed, a full mouth tasting penance.

Remember it when you are afraid.
The platform and the carriage pulled apart
and you were pushed beyond your calling and yourself
into a momentary lack of grace;
into a girl who put her mouth to yours
and made you take the penance off her tongue.

Comfort yourself.
Remember it like this.

Delta

Open your eyes.
A parched bandage is uncoiling on your arm.
You feel no pain, no fear: your brain
has been drawn out with hooks, preserved in alcohol.
You are merely the kernel of a wooden shell,
but I am here, in the gloom, the frail rushlight,
the suggestion of spears, chariot wheels,
the small longboat at your feet.
Bronze mirrors lean like a corridor.
Don't be deceived. This is a sealed room.

Lie down and wait.
Comfort yourself with dreams.
Sand will go on sifting itself into a recessed door
but, in time, a dome raised cubits high
will open on familiar sky. Yes. It will.
A caravan will pass, returning home.
Believe yourself in it, a traveller, moving
among those who sell food at the roadside,
among the gaudy stalls of beads, rugs, nets...

Listen.
There is music, water on the floodtide,
ibis and white geese rising
rowdy as Cleethorpes gulls. Hold this thought
and you have Calor gas seeping sweet as mildew
in a tomb; an umbrella, pushchair, skateboard
propped against a brown formica partition.

Lie down and wait.
Consider your knees. A pyramid in the sheet.
Your arm. No longer embalmed but burned
last night when you were frying fish,
too pissed to read the zigzag hieroglyphs
of a car-battery telly...
Pursue this fantasy. It may release you.

Strawberries

'The man in the wilderness said to me,
How many strawberries grow in the sea?'

Here on the sea bed we're eating
strawberries and salt, not counting
punnets. Answering to the likes of him
you could go daft or drown, go in
over your head. Underwater fruit
is all maroon, sea-cured and tart;
it ripens in the undertow –
gravid trawlers break nets on it, go
aground. I tell him cloven tails, singing
mermaids on the rocks – tell him nothing
grows in sea, all roots begin in broken
earth. He says, Ask a silly question.
All right, Smartarse. Just say how many
barrels. Be precise. Don't get funny.

'I answered him as I thought good,
As many red herrings as grow in the wood.'

(The Whole Duty of Man, 1773)

33

Felix

For you the pavement is sparklers and smashed puddles.
Your breath haloes, you dance, grimacing,
two-stepping dogshit, late for school again.
Your sister is too snooty even to glance;
her shoes remain unscathed. You career
from gutter to railings, I-spying fantasy
letters we can never guess.

C for condoms, you shout and search my face.
To do with kissing, something for girls.
You kick the wreckage, shuffling flaccid skins.
I start distracting, steering you away.
A party. Soon. Ask your friends, to celebrate
when you were born... the shock of your red hair
and you, piercingly alert, eyes like frost

behind a tearing caul... Like plastic, you suggest,
like clingfilm, so I'll never drown or die.
More like these, I think, for safety and for luck.
Dickhead, your sister whispers in your happy face.

Laundry

A woman in a yard at night does certain things:
she drags a sheet down off the line,
laps one on one along her arm,
half listens to familiar sounds;
a dog; turning out time at the pub;
some man's fragmented song.

A bedroom light might ladder on the wall;
she reaches blind, preoccupied,
because it's there, full pelt but fine,
delicate as cat and mouse, desperate
as cat and tail: who'll watch her back?

She trails hems, snags them on a hedge;
tests for dampness with her lips,
drops pegs, daren't bend to pick them up.

She hears something sliding in an upstairs room;
silence unrolling easy as a rug.
The kitchen flares, squaring the window
like a screen: someone enters barefoot
in a revealing shift, dignified,
sea-horse absurd. Looks out
and steams the glass. A launderette

where women dance unasked, take corners
according to the rules, pass back and back,
fold edge to edge. The phone rings twice.

She frees another sheet, winds it
on the others. Comes back, inhaling dark,
avoiding bikes, a pram, marbles underfoot.
Upstairs, children sleep in litters,
sharing beds with friends. In here, a fridge,

a basket of unwashed things, a small table,
a clock, unmoved, five minutes fast,
a guest who'll be no use, no help,
her hands full, lifting curtains,
rattling locks, her sweet mouth out of sync
with all this mumbling about going home.

Confinement

That winter the stairs were always unlit.
Home late from work, I'd feel my way,
unlock the door by touch
and before I pressed the switch look up, wait
to see my lamp put out a saucer to the dark.

The skylight was almost clear then,
night came down to it at once,
a movement quick and weighty as water.

At first I'd count you by the moon, by my own fingers,
half believing I could feel you in my skin.
Then it snowed for weeks, accumulating on the glass,
filtering a tracing paper air. A diffuse frost
charged the constant underwater I crossed and crossed
mindless as a swimmer, keeping time for you.

At night, in the cold sheets, unable to sleep
I began to count you in days and hours,
I named you, held your head, your feet,
felt you turn in my own body heat.

Tonight, you've slept for twenty years.
I leave an overheated house, go out
into the cold backyard for air.
A neighbour calls me to the fence to watch.
He's opening the ice on his pond. The fish come up
preserved by their cold blood, their trust.

I close a frozen room on you, your placid drowning face.
and listen to my neighbour, who has learned to wait,
obedient to the rules that govern living things.
We share a cigarette and then discuss
the nature of confinement and release.

Pharmacy

Tonight in the vaults of the hospital,
in the tea-break between four am and half past
we read the scrawled transcriptions
of healing formulae; considering
the measurements *nocte* and *per diem*.

Tonight we hear
or imagine we hear above us
the unoiled wheels, voices
and their echo, refined,
curtailed; a series of swing doors.

No one comes down; they pass through
prone, mounded in red blankets,
memorising their own fine sweat,
inset neon, a reversed silver watch,
the crushed hand of a nurse.

Transported on waves of pethidine
between admission and intensive care,
between the active labour ward
and the abrupt delivery of a frozen child,
no one. Tonight the vaults are quiet,

harshly lit, waiting to mediate
between the business of casualty
and the upper corridors, between
the turned back sheets, white aertex covers
of a half dark sleeping ward,

the *little something, dear*
to put you out. Tonight
the cushioned feet scuff overhead
unheard; the vacant lift comes down
and we retrieve the labelled packages,

a clipboard of prescriptions, invoices,
and, in your starched pocket for later,
a stapled wedge of tissue memoranda.

Voice

Call, by all means, but just once
don't use the *broken heart again* voice;
the *I'm sick to death of life and women
and romance* voice *but with a little help
I''ll try to struggle on* voice

Spare me the promise and the curse
voice, the ansafoney *Call me, please
when you get in* voice, the *nobody knows
the trouble I've seen* voice; the *I'd value
your advice* voice.

I want the how it was voice;
the *call me irresponsible but aren't I nice* voice;
the *such a bastard but I warn them in advance* voice.
The *We all have weaknesses
and mine is being wicked* voice

the *life's short and wasting time's
the only vice* voice, the *stay in touch,
but out of reach* voice. I want to hear
the *things it's better not to broach* voice
the *things it's wiser not to voice* voice.

Mine Host

I had a name but they have swallowed it,
downed it by the pint. And I have swallowed
so much that I might give way. I might.

Tonight, I just contain myself. I go on
pulling ale and nodding Aye and Gerraway?
with one ear cocked against the margin
of a conversation, on the edge
of mild debate and brewing trouble.

I have the punchlines, the final say,
Time, gents. Sup up. It's Time.
And they subside, obedient, cowed:

I shepherd the unsteady, hold the door.
And someone might catch hell outside,
someone at home might come it, question
what's been spent, someone might wonder
what I buy one half so precious as I sell...

I slam the bolts behind. I touch hands,
gently, with myself and rock and sing
I wish I loved the human race, I wish...

I tilt my head, Yes, my good man? Yes, Sir
Yes? Yes? Sometimes it will not pass.
The juke box dies. A glass of rum and black
burns sanctuary and in my mirrors
in my bottles me and me

and my cathedral settles.
Then I bucket the fag ends and ashes,
wipe the bar and spread the towels;
I gather up the dregs and slops
and tip them in my special cup.

A Matter of Respect

My father was a baker. Dapper by day,
skilled, useful. I recall him, breathless
from the ovens; skin pallid with flour
and weariness. His dark bereaved eyes.
He came home at dawn, lay in a narrow bed
alone. She thought him soft as dough.

I stand on the back step in white, breathe
fresh air when my work's complete.
Behind me, everything in reverse. A mirror,
close enough to kiss or bite, remains
unmisted, clear. There is no heat in me
but there is craft in gauze and spool,

the law of generations in my hands.
His art lay in giving life to yeast,
mine in levelling the risen and the meek.
What I knead and stretch and pack,
others bake, see consumed. I've no truck
with corruption. My pleasure lies in tact.

They're brought to me – vacant, aphasic, distilled.
Some taken in time, at the mercy only
of their own lives. Some ravaged, faces peeled,
scalps lidded, pillaged. I hide a running stitch
in new washed hair. 'Too formal. Not her style.'
I stand back, discreet. 'Peaceful. Could be

asleep.' This is my reward. Their error.
I offer a half smile, condolences, my hand.
The numb accept it, made courteous by grief;
the quick leave it untouched. I could say
Au revoir. She said, 'No guts. No life in him.'
I anoint and soothe. Make amends, reparation.
This is the precise meaning of revenge.

A Man Will Always Talk

A man will always talk openly to a woman
once he is convinced of her frigidity or her sophistication.
COLETTE

These orientals have the right idea, he says.
You seize on the story of the zen master
who, in answer to a question,
pushed his prize pupil into the mud...

He studies you, blank as a jury
already under the spell of his next verdict.
What question? he wants to know.
You consider pushing him off his stool.

Now, the Chinese... he taps his glass,
take their songbirds into the gardens
at evening to show them the flowers,
the setting sun reflected among the reeds...

Lovely, you agree, but he is grimacing
into his beer. He can't be fooled.
It's all chemicals and bubbles.
You tell yourself a joke about bars and reflection.

Me, he says, *I'm a long distance swimmer.*
Endurance. Ten lengths a day, rain or shine,
at the new baths. Tones me up. Yes, of course.
Water is your element, air would kill you,

earth and fire I have already discounted
and this illusion of a common purpose
can't even support an evening's drinking.
He nods, twice, *Do any sport yourself?*

You weigh the ice-bucket against the ashtray
and say 'Chinese mud wrestling
every evening shine or rain
out in the garden.'

Oh yes? he smiles.
A perfect combination of the two, these lads.
Masters of the rigid form. Haiku. Tankas.
And you can't beat them when it comes to explosives.

Frances J: *Self-Portrait 1896*

That mild winter, late November
you dismissed your staff,
shut your door against friends, family,
gentlemen callers, and sat up to the hearth
not really reading, not thinking,
outwaiting the short days;
your whole life balanced on a gift
you thought you had, a talent
for the things that change
with the solstice, the shift towards
another year, I began in earnest...

A fair enough likeness
but grainy, half profile –
in truth, it's mainly shoulder,
pearls, a loop of cambric petticoat,
broderie anglaise, a silk foot,
a drooping bony hand and there,
between the index and the thumb,
your cigarette, the curving inch of ash.

How was it for you
to sit all night all winter
the fire dying out –
why mend it and sit down again,
an ankle rested on a knee,
an elbow on a thigh
a new preoccupation with technique...
this rigid pose, your face
towards a mantel shelf
of framed impassive faces,
moustached, hard collared
empty faces. *Soon.*
Perhaps in this new year...

It seems you'd cast too many spells by then
and it was too late to recant. *I want.*
Two Boston galleries, a retrospective
and the best of your new work.

I wake and sleep, half dressed, prepared...
Late spring, they'd sifted your papers,
put your affairs in order: *just this:*
my work, one man, and for the rest
six feet of solid wall.

Dormant

An owl killed something, at length, in the garden
under his window and there was no one to turn to
in that broad bed, no one to pester awake,
Hold me. Take me away from the dark.
No one *I'm here. It's all right.* No one
the state of you, you're not fit to be out.
Just the continuing heat, the sash up
all night, and sound translated, carried in
on the unbroken country dark. His own hand,
unfamiliar to his face, his mouth.
Afraid to put on the light, afraid to sleep.
Twice he'd dreamed
an impossible vantage point above the roof;
canted gaping slates, beams bowed and separated

to allow him in, the boards sprung and giving
under his feet. Not damp rot, but moist:
the joists above him, closing and in his palms,
splinters; his hands closing, wilfully, spitefully,
on them and behind him cold and silence...
Each time he'd woken to his mother's house,
her pleasant morning voice, the radio;
a heat haze hanging in the lower valley,
over dried out pasture: a clear view
of his father close by the house,

cuffs turned back, a blue shirt open to the waist,
mending walls, or, smaller on the hill,
evenly turning square spades of earth,
burying a lamb? placenta? Working.
In the swing back dressing table mirror,
his face, tanned, a little thinner;
in the walnut wardrobe door
a disembodied arm, a sleeve
dull white. Dark cords. Go home.
Decide. A leasehold farmer?

On this, his last day,
he took his book, his cigarettes, a mug of tea,
and settled on the step. Midday, the dogs came down

to lie nose over nose on the porch,
dozing fretfully, whimpering.
Sheep loitered at the gate, watching.
And on the sill behind him
a bee, yellow velcro belly up
rearing intermittently, refusing,
drawing on a faulty connection.

Between them, they drove him out
into the fields, to a corner of long grass
where he lay down and smoked
and absently picked scales of sunburn
from his chest. Complex, unique, priceless
cells. He held them one by one to the light.
Finally, he slept. And woke, remembering
So. Just tell me this. Who will hold you
in that fly-blown hall of mirrors ,
who'll lie between you and your illness?

He walked down to the house, entered
for once by the front door. Banisters
filtered motes and grains into the dark.
Picture frames and glass. Movement.
Thin carpet. Shifting whorls
of anaglypta under his fingers. And here,
between him and the source of light,
his mother, a small shadow,
her hurt unsteady courtesy
'Your friend called twice. He'd taken a drink.

It's no excuse for rudeness...' Twice. That broad owl face,
those slow dilated eyes. *Run home to your mother's,*
the ice-queen's summer palace. Retreat if you must.
Convalesce. I'll leave you in peace. Michael
called me twice? He spoke then and when she turned away,
he put his hand to her shoulder, her closed face,
her cracked grey eyes, her loss. And his, the years
of cold accumulated honesty.
For himself, he kept the dreams,
pure as coincidence and how the angel of mercy speaks in them
with such a patient predatory wooing voice
Listen, my better half, love of my life,
for the likes of us there is no proper time or place.

Felix, 11

What it amounts to is this;
you, in a box, somewhere
near the park I guess, anxious
about the new number, the proper coins,
just enough to cover thirty seconds
of the thirty miles between us

Mum. Dad said to call and say
I landed home all right
and the dog's eaten the phone again
and I'll see you soon
*and to say...*you hesitate, worried,
Oh, yes.   And thank you for having me.

The ansaphone clicks off, spares me
the price of a new life, the cost
of *Felix, you're welcome, anytime,*
just be my guest.

Solicitor

Looking for trouble,
he's brought her a double vodka.
Not her drink but *after all*
your tastes can alter
and she takes it without argument
to displease him, to confirm
their strangeness.
           He circles
and settles for a corner seat.
They drink in silence.
It's familiar, this pause
before the proper phrase,
the precise consideration
of necessary loss, unjust enrichment,

A legal concept or a moral imperative?
She's lost now in the tangle of hard words,
the warm underwater air, this crowded bar
but coming to her senses
just as he is going under
for the last time, searching out
the proper terms.
           My solicitor
will speak to your solicitor.
The last weeks, the last days
of a lifelong marriage. He tries it
on his tongue, probing
and finds no leverage, nothing
to release them; no balance between
the heart broken and the heart
broken open.
           You never had a ring.
Accept this as a small token. A negative,
smaller than a celebration stamp;
three children, their heads together,
smiling. He puts his finger on the rim
of her glass: *Another? Have you time?*

The Trick with the Pillar of Salt

Sidestep the angel on the porch,
brush off warnings, pleas, the magic ring
and run.

Let vases go green breeding sweetness,
lights burn to nothing
the boiler make good its threat.
Begone

with nothing but a generous coat,
a plastic bag for form's sake, empty
but a grand design and handles
you've made double sure
in tight unsliding knots.

Your father's name has faded in the book.
Assume a title of your own.
Listen hard but do not look,
you'll hear it soon; the front door
chipping at the lock. In time
some random draught will marry hasp and frame.

You've cut the key that doesn't fit.
Now turn the key that will not turn.

Vermeer's Woman

A room opening into other rooms.
A window, a table, a woman pouring milk,
dreaming, shaping a love letter,
weighing a six month belly light;

caught in coloured air she is
confined and celebrated,
a madonna even in the brothel
to a man who loves women, placid
round bodied, composed.

Sometimes it's true.
She's handling something like silk –
his skin or cream; words come,
a small fist opening on the heart,
a first flutter in the ribs –

but mostly she curses, *Why*
are you always in my space.
When can I sit, be quiet.
She dips that cowled face, hooded eyes,
will not look up.

Nude in a Red Armchair

You know the pose:
one hand cupping the face
one inverted, pointing away
an eye dilating on flake white, blind
to the floor, his shifting feet,
the other cornered, full of light.
Where you aren't shaved, you're dyed,
even your breasts can't agree;
your thighs are clenched and wide –
it takes three short lines to open them.
You know the weight of beads on skin
the purr of velvet on your back
your own name
say it, say this chair is brown
and I am naked.

The Peeing Woman, 1965

Not brushstrokes, oils
but cunning doorways
to the real world:
firm to the threshold

but opened, entered,
they dissolved,
became amorphous, vacuous.
Years, he struggled,

concealed keys in rugs, tablecloths,
curtains – an interlock of teeth
and boxes, an encoded index
read and diagnosed

as illness. Absurd as his fear
of waking on the wrong side
of the mattress, coming to
in her coma, clenched

under a low brow,
a peculiar ungiftedness,
a varnished unfamiliar finger
to his mouth. Tasteless.

She brought roses, orchids,
oranges. She offered herself,
soft, scented, round.
He remained polite, lost

somewhere in the infinite
recess of his own art, exiled.
But the dispossessed inherit
patience. They wait, believing

talent will out. Home.
And the first night
he'll pose and paint her;
his wives, that woman

who yawned and drained him.
Her lips, her mouths
additional to his. Dismembered,
double headed, lop breasted, alert.

Squared. And life so sweet, cubic,
he almost laughs.
His genius. A miracle
he's not melted in this bath.

When you are cold at night

listening, memorising
the shelf, the grille, the exact grain of the wall
the never-stillness, tedium
knotted in a threat of riot
of someone breaking
on a careless letter, a bad visit,

I am here and waking too.
I connect your face
and lose it in fragments
month to month.
I spin out your laughter
weave it around old jokes.
Sometimes it breaks.
You say, It's like a conversation
carried on while I'm in the kitchen
making tea that nobody wants.
You're right, but it's small talk,
it falters, runs one-sided, waiting.

We are careful, tongue-tied,
too much between us on a table
made wide enough for fingertips to meet
if we can stretch and someone turns away.
I learn your mouth again, your hands.
The rest is mime.
When you are cold at night
I am here and waking too,
watching a kettle boil and boil
into the air, going dry.

Alibi

I have the quarry to myself on Sunday.
It's always cold up here, even in summer,
even in the shelter. Open sky is graced, made fancy,
by red and blue graffiti on the glass.
I smoke slowly just to make it last.
This early, there's nothing on the road.

When it rains I listen: birds faltering,
going silent, my own peculiar pulse.
I watch limestone walls darken from the edge,
the path softens, absolved in coins, hosts, plates.

These mornings I can live with all the white.

Who loves, who wants to tell, marked on the door,
same initials on the bench, *Forever. True.*
Reliable as Joe Pavlowski, solemn as a seraph
at the gate, giving me a hand over the fence,
then his altar boy smile and all I need to know –
the sermon; any untoward events: *a dog came in;*

*our Jimmy took collection; we've to pray
for Connie Kelly; your Dominic never showed;*
which of my aunts turned out for early mass;
a palm leaf knotted in a cross – no charge to you –
or that once only offer, sworn sighting of me
in a back pew, *face it, you're sunk anyway.*

I walk two miles, the long way round,
to hang my coat in the hall and wait.
The radio flares, shuts off. My dad comes out,
his shoes a hard glove on one hand,
the other muffled in a rag –

That Walter Gabriel. He shakes his head, laughs.
My mother hobbles down in stockinged feet,
her hat already pinned in place,

Now, she says, giving me a long look,
Don't you feel all the better for that.

A Champion Send-Off

They were all done up like bouncers
but I was despatched to answer the door.
It was Joan in the astrakhan and leather and the boys.
She kissed me through a steam of White Fire
and they shouldered past,

surly studs with sharp haircuts and bright earrings.
I wondered about the jigsaws we'd sent
last christmas... *It's a bad do*, she told me,
doing a quick scan of the hallway
for the dahlias she'd sent,

turning the wreaths to read the cards,
straightening her hat in the mirror,
It's an awful thing...
Can't do with dahlias, my dad muttered,
They harbour earwigs. But I like them earrings.

It's a bad do, someone was telling my mother.
How are you keeping it's been a long while.
I'm bearing up. My mother always knows the form
and she put out a steady hand
and offered tea or sherry? A relief

to be sent out for extra milk,
measuring my steps in what was still early morning,
cool time to think, smart in the new shoes and coat.
He'd pressed the money on me.
'Listen here and just think on.

It's only right. They have these capers
just so every bugger can be dressed to death.'
When I came back there were more of them,
standing so as not to crease the best suits, easing fingers
under new collars, stroking borrowed ties.

Tell them to sit down, my dad said, Stood about.
Makes it feel like closing time...
The sunshine kept edging round the curtains,
out of place in the underwater air,
motes lighting on the shelves

we'd cleared for mass cards, flowers, documents,
but my brother was anxious. They'll be here.
Any time now. Kathleen was calm,
leaning from her chair, knees pressed white
in a tube of black suede skirt,

tacking Mary's sagging hem. My dad shook his head.
Take it off lass. Else you're sewing sorrow to your back.
The needle was away long before they drew up outside,
my dad leading on the conveyor belt of hearses,
boxed, stately as any of us

who shuffled into the proper order,
status given to close family. Chief moaners first,
he winked us out, You're giving me
a champion send-off. The Co-op no less.
And it's a bit of divi for your poor old mother...

Just give over now, I thought.
If I start laughing, dad,
they'll think that I'm gone daft with all the grief.
To hell with them, he said. In fact I'll have a word
with somebody down here this very afternoon.

Bird

Backing out of Leeds
on the late running 18.26
leaving the glittering Armley skyline,
the grey unlit castle, and here in the sidings,
a solitary stop-out magpie.
I'm ignorant of wild life
but I know that they're unlucky
and tribal and dapper – every nightclub bouncer,
that preening strut, the head one side, wings tucked in,
and he's there judging and sampling
the back tyre of something low slung
in the executive car park,
his beak opening, covetous and damaging.

Me, I'm a graduate, you said,
of Doctor Silky's School for Suavers.
The lines that never fail. A woman
on each arm and one for best.
Caroline. Rebecca. Rose.
The rest all Alice.
Pour me another, Alice. Now take the head off it.
Don't worry, Alice. Don't think
that you're just cunt to me.
You reckon I've got no respect?

But generous to a fault with cash and drink
and diamante until that Christmas
an alice bit a rival's finger to the bone
and off, and you dived in to catch the ring.
Slags, you said. And barred them both.

Reflected, one cocked predatory eye
in the steel trim, the mirror
he can't release or carry.
A frailty, after all, dependence
on the tribe, the inbred appetite?

Inside, you have no time for alices.
They let you down. They grass.
On visits, they just cry and show you up.
No class. Not like your own. The lads.
I close now, hoping this leaves me
as I found you today; detained
but still equipped to fly,
still arguing the black and white,
considering what we might reject.
Take care. Your everloving aunt.

Done with Mirrors
(for Patrick Brian)

There are tricks of memory, sleights
of hand. Histories; the one alleged,
the one they know for sure and won't admit,
the one they'd never recognise. Hard fact.

Downstairs. Now. Somewhere in this house,
their mother, not happy but singing as if she were;
their father, deeper, point and counterpoint,
the child hunched on the stairs,
the boy who hugs her, blocks her ears. Come away.
Forget it. The Irish are all fucking mad.
Smile. Smile at the bad word, repeat it...

He shrugs himself into the overcoat, settles it;
his hands, much like her own, fisted in the pockets.
How tired he looks. Old. Their mother's green flecked eyes,
her mouth, the songs. Present. Keep it
to the present tense: an edge of cuff, his wrist,
and up the sleeve the blue 2 Para fading out
above her tattooed names spelled right...

        In my father's house
I have inherited the kitchen. You're just another guest in it.
Don't spar with me. Don't rummage in the things
I've put away. History

a back bedroom, the door locked.
Under them, the house wrecked. Everyone exploded, gone.
Nothing in the world but him. Never. It was never true.
I know, he said, You're Sugar Ray, I'm Rocky Marciano.
Come on, girl. Box me, hit me, aim for the chin. Come on.

You've not done bad, he says, And are you spoken for?
Vaguely, he has it somewhere. An envelope, her note,
the photo he folded and lost, confetti tipped out
on an army blanket *he's English. Heathen.*
Perhaps she never wrote it...History

the held peace, flesh of my flesh, loyalty
bred in the bone... *mainly in the kneecaps*
he says, *mainly*... and in the bloodline
a spread of venom, a trace of cornered rat,
you never ever cross your own, *that family shite.*

The times she'd watched his back, times
they'd both been pelted out to mass,
the one time she'd stood her ground...
            Sweet Sugar Ray you lovely little mover,
tender as a bruise...hit me, fight me, kid. Come on.
Something cold and hard, impacted in a ricochet
from wall to bed to bed. Weave. Evade. Training,
he said, Because life's hard. 'Compared to what?'
He decked her for her clever mouth. Learn
to button it...

        Sit down, she says,
you make it feel like closing time. Sit down.
He'll stand. *You were just a kid. You'll not recall*
THEIR DAD: How come the Irish can't forget?
THEIR MOTHER: How come the English can't remember?

DIALOGUE: Here, kid. Aim for the chin.

Defensive, divided and sick to death of it...
in my father's house...even then, domestic
decisive as a breadknife, angled to open up
a direct line. Come away. Forget it.
The shape, the texture
of a blue breast pocket, a stain, the colour
of a ten bob note unfolding in it.
His outdated currency, her territory:

Sit down with me. Try the other hand to hand.
Aren't we the same mixed breed, haven't we the impulse
towards speech, to what reflects and keeps
at bay a recognition of hard fact? Hard
as a first incision to say, Let it go.
Have sense. That stuff's all in the past.

Market

(for Janice Rose)

Imagine you are a lonely bullfrog
crying out in the wilderness.
Yoko Ono said that
but not to me.

Is that yourself stood there?
he shouted across St Stephen's Square.
It wasn't me again
but I got the drift.

It's a bit of a bugger, she'd said,
eyeing the grand display of china –
Haven't I always my hands full
when I spot something fancy?

Tell you what. We'll come back.
We'll make a special journey
for pisspots and pancheons...
Yes, I thought. We will.

And between us we hefted the carriers
of caulies and cabbages, backed off
from the lovely fragile things.
We'll be back, she said. When the fine day comes.

But he leaned over the market stall,
Missis. Is that any sort of a way to be talking?
A woman using language.
And in front of a girl as well.

Listen, she said on the bus home, I'll tell you
about the whistling woman and the crowing hen.
Your ears'll take a lot of shite
but your mouth's your own.

Duty

You hated France. Its day on dismal day
of pelting rain, the price, the cold,
the tedious sober grey of it.
Each disappointment told like beads,
your disillusion clutched,
a hard won holy medal. You're cheated
and I'm sorry. The dye dripping
from your skirt, your flight delayed,
your umbrella lost or worse. I'm sorry.
My face is stiff with it. I'm awkward
with your tea, your cigarette; relieved
you'd not want me to kiss you better.

You're head down, rummaging your bag,
dredging small foreign coins. I almost miss
These French. Your father's people...
and hard on it, *Here. Don't say I never...*
Your gift. Not duty frees, not wine
but water in a plastic dome, a bluish slosh
of Eau de Grotte de Lourdes. I tilt it back
and clear the Holy Mother's drenched
implacable and English face.

Impediment

Sunday morning after early mass,
Ruby Murray on the radio,
an aunt up to the elbows
in a sinkful of cabbage
and us jostling, virtuous,
armed with kitchen knives and peelers
aiming to pocket one or two
of the peapods or the smaller carrots –
Aunt Eileen it was,
last of the big romantics
Won't you just listen to that husk?
And isn't she singing there
on the back of a terrible impediment?

Not having the word, we agreed
and she went on to tell us how
one way or another aren't all of us crippled
and is it not right after all –
we nodded – that the lame man
saved the drowning pig
and his crutches as it came to pass
served several purposes
not least to lift him
between Mooney's and the singing side
at Rafferty's, whereon
he told the tale
and so inspired, we hope to God,
a multitude?

What's left of that day; steam and smoke
a wet of whiskey for us all before we ate,
the vague anxiety of the imagined weight
of our grandfather's boot, a heel rested
on the dog's head – a dog precisely to the hour
my own age but without breeding,
not in the proper tradition
of the O'Hara thoroughbreds;
a mongrel, faithful and content
to sleep under his master's foot;

nowhere to go, nothing much to do
until the family tabby might elect
to claw his placid head
and hook his dozy eye out just for sport.

I'm left with how the drink
and then the politics broke out
and how the aunts were dextrous
with the china and the glasses,
how the cloth whisked off
and we were ushered out by them
and in by Martin
who'd have us sing with him *Bold Fenian Men*
and out again by Kathleen
who offended us with *only children*.

The older cousins listened at the door
and soothed us in the kitchen,
fed us cake and trifle by the fistful
until the gramaphone came on
and we filed back, subdued
to *Josef Locke* who had *the good man's fault*
and owed the queen a fierce debt,
They talked, we listened
for the inbred frailty, the useful just impediment.

Him Downstairs

(for Gladys Ruth Sansom)

We shut a door, he slams one off its hinges.
We vacuum, he sandblasts his ceiling.
We poke the fire, he sets his place alight –
sirens and searchlights and hoses
and us on the street in our vests all night.
Months of peace, we forget him.
Then one of us smiles and he has hysterics –
we put the telly on, the stereo to drown the howling –
and he's got an organ, electric, the last word
in speakers and he'll lift the floorboards practising...

A finger to the lips; he's under us, aping.
No harm done. But it's the parties,
weddings, funerals, birthdays, ours,
and he's down there bouncing off the walls,
chit-chatting, boogieing with himself,
smoking three fags at a time,
eating fit to burst, breaking glasses,
offering himself out, holding his own jacket...

We do nothing, say nothing,
just nod in the street to be civil
and pray he'll move out or go mad or die.
We've tried. One New Year, we'd had about enough –
Auld Lang Syne bawled out,
louder, two beats behind us
and the terrible kissing, the resolutions,
the family phone-calls. Enough.

We went down there to sort it
once and for all. Hammering,
pounding his chimes off the wall –
and through his letterbox, Come on then,
just answer this bloody door;
and him rattling the chain, battering the inside,
practically through it with his boot, shouting
I know you're there, open up or I'm coming out.

Possession

I have the narrow view, focused on a sky
that doesn't change; when clouds come
they fill the screen, a mottled face,
and then I walk about like anyone,
speak openly without excuse, without appeal,

until they've gone. I have one room. It's enough,
it holds me, but once I was afraid
I'd been misplaced, left without language or redress,
a statement in my mouth like a flat stone
I daren't spit out or open with my tongue.

Silence made me brave; I thought of you
and swallowed hard, let it fall inside.
Now it moves, a regular and pointed metronome,
a constant and increasing rap that opens,
then discounts the soft and bloody that I need to live.
Beaten smooth and heartless from the inside out,
I'm safe and you are safe, inside the cavity:

the room I lose when I wake up.
I think the sky was always narrow
and I was always greedy for it, a fledgling
wanting to be fed. I admit this, but, truly,
I've forgotten everything before, everything
except this room above the fence, above the trees.

One night the floorboards buckled, branches drove up
and through and spread, soundless as fingers
on these cramped walls. I walked the broken floor.
I set my feet in knuckled roots,
braced my shoulders, let the tree accept my weight;
I set my face against the light and chose
the space between the glitter and the glass.
Of course, there were the tricks I save for fantasy,
details, a skirt caught up on twigs,
your hands full of blouse and flesh

but what I use is this: how my eyelids closed
on emptiness and it was negative and rich;
how I became the brittle scattered sound of leaves
and you became my wish, attainable and granted, easy as a kiss.

This place was put aside for me to be alone.
I can't be alone. I wait, uncertain as all lovers,
racked by hesitation and unease;
dark is the small reprieve before sleep takes me
like a common thief. I don't protest.
I've learned to welcome what is, after all, release.

I am returned here, untidy and bewildered as a ransacked house,
unable to regain the boundary, the real wall.
Then I stand up on the bed, remind myself
that morning comes as fog through a fine mesh fence.
It blurs the lawns, the cheap green promise
of an open prison. Shrubs and cornered rockeries
are interlocked by razor wire, its simple shine
discreet as good jewellery.
I look down on those who exercise in pairs,

on those who break the ranks
merely to smoke and saunter on the edge;
sometimes it seems I recognise you there and I step down
and back into my surface life, no more imprisoned
with you than I am in dreams.

Now it is quiet as someone listening

someone who loves you and cannot speak.
There have been flurries all day,
the sky cut by phone wires
sags against the ceiling, watermarked –
gulls fall upwards
turn like autumn ash-keys. It is spring
but it will not let go.

A jug of daffodils holds all the light,
there are thin plates, white
with violets at the rim.
She brings two bowls. You see
the shadow of her fingers,
soup, yellow as wine and hot,
a surface film reflecting only steam,
dark bread, a polished crust she breaks.
The centre gives like cake.

Later you lean together at the sink.
It starts to rain, it may be sleet.
She tells you, If it snows tonight
I shall be happy right through.

The isle is full of noises

The isle is full of noises,
sounds and sweet airs that give delight and hurt not.
THE TEMPEST

Mornings, you wake into a hush,
the steady lull of rain, a shushing
undertone of tide. Eternal daylight
where you are, and dawn a simple stain...

You write it, I'll drip wax on it.
This early my hands are still unsteady,
it's dark enough for candles here,
but I can still decipher in your careful hand
the discipline of what is given, what is held,
the reticent and hardened priest in you.
I notice Old McConnell's out
and Calum with him, hunched up in the prow.
Not a civil word between them all day long
but they'll haul in half a hundredweight...

All spring we've had the rain in common
but sometimes I'm dry, landlocked
in old recurring dreams, trudging powdered grooves
that once rocked rivers end to end,
breaking through a tedious wickerwork
of trees, to kneel and rake
an aimless channel in the dust...

I tell you this, knowing you'll rise to it;
the usual jokes about my scrawl,
a half meant swipe at women and at alcohol
and there between *our fruitful conflict*
and your *do write soon* you have addressed
the problem. Mine. *Thirst and grains and barrenness?*
You're built on sand, my friend.

Mornings, you wake at peace. Contained.
Your seaboard and your croft, your boxy bed,
yourself. All safe. *Come up and stay.*
It's heaven on earth.
        God grant me, but not yet.
Your faith's in rock and mine runs through
the underhand of dreams. I offer you the salt,
the shells, the tiny teeming fish,
brittle bones picked clean of flesh.
To mention flesh is fighting talk
where we come from

but down here, I have mornings
when I wake with him. Our arms, our legs
a supple interweave, we drift together
in this bed, drawn in the undertow
of sleep and common sweat. And I am happy
to forget just where my boundaries lie;
spread wider than the world, my own hand
in my mouth, I bite down blind.

I can't say that I miss you much,
but write to me. I search your letters
for what I most need; the blessing
of a slow abrading sea, its union
with a stony island base, the dissolution
in each hard remorseless kiss.

St Jude's

It is the start of a long summer
that will take them through to October
and this is one of the idle aimless days
she'll remember best

for its quiet and its heat,
an afternoon in a cliff top garden,
where no one will come to call them home.
Free to sit together in the sun,

she reads and smokes, he sleeps,
his heat-rashed hand turned slack in hers,
his foot turned out onto the path.
The shadow of her head, her arm,

the fanned pages of a novel,
a coil of cigarettes and leaves. This bench,
this dried out tree and generations
At Peace At Rest. Their pitted slabs,

their names mean nothing,
Treasured memories   Beloved son
their dates, a code of absence in the stone.
Nothing here for the living

among *Two years   Six months*;
these shortened plots, the finite strategy
of someone else's art, much like the rusted rails,
the carved lych gate, his perfect half moon nails.

She nods to the man in shorts
who wheels his bike, leans it
on a grave and kneels to work.
Dahlias, a jar of water, *Beloved daughter*.

Routinely, without warning, the tide
beneath them, opens its wide reach on shell
and bone and sodden wood. A hoard
of jetsam it prepares to beach. *Sleep on*.

The drawn scream of a gull.
An old warped door pulled to.
If you surface now, my love, you'll rise
into what's passed and gone. Sleep on.

Once, before him, she was narrow,
channelled to one end.
She couldn't pass a wishing well,
a church, *Give me. I must have.*

She eases his face against her shoulder
as if she were the pietà, the mother
between him and what might come,
Between my children and all harm...

She learned to pray most carefully
in places such as this
In your mercy. By your good grace.
Intercede for me, Saint Jude.

Patron of the hopeless, women without pride,
Grant me, in time, a living child,
the even rise of his chest,
his warm breath, a steady pulse.

February, Bradford Photography Museum

Crushed between David, Tom and Katherine
we're on a hard bench, learning
how the earth moves, how we're placed
between the sickle moon,
the full moon, named unexplored planets,
the insignificant and burned out stars.

We stop at the windows between floors
to point out the beauty of the snow,
miles of plate glass melted into flurries,
and here, a fragile wet membrane settled
on a litter bin, a blackened brittle tree.
Our common breath, our warm fingers

clear a series of small circles.
We tell them all we know between us,
of the unique and priceless nature
and the appearance of crystals.
They question us about tomorrow,
extract promises about sledges, snowballs.

I've lost the timetable. Transport home
is anybody's guess but we offer certainties
and stories about bleak nights we've survived
on Leeds Kings Cross Wakefield station.
Listen. Trust us. Your hand closes over mine.
Tom, one step ahead, rests his face,

his tongue on the banister. Our knuckles slide
on spit and varnish up two flights, towards
the continuous video of the hand
of the sleeping man at the summer picnic:
creased living tissue, every pulse and cell
held loosely but opened to us, observed,

and his partner beside him,
her knees, her fingers locked in his...
The children are bored, they want
drinks and food, they want the man's hand
to *do* something. They want him awake.
They wonder how deep the snow is now.

A nasal droning voice informs us
that we're complex clustered molecules
and we hear again how simply planets turn,
how easy blood and water shifts
and spreads, an ocean or a small stain
on a skirt. The kids want warmth

and sleep, the fast train home.
Soon, we say, hurrying them across the dark,
through the city, over frost lit streets
to the station *Soon* – as if time
were in our gift, not a continuum
of lifelong chance and miracles and loss,

don't slip and *haven't I told you...*
they laugh and mimic us *a hundred million times*
look where you're going, hold hands.

Trousseau

You turn the sheet down, knowing
she'll be impressed. Hospital tucks
and a monogram no less. Fifty pence
on the market, from a basket of rags

in need of mending but real Belfast linen
and these initials – *yours and his* –
her thumbnail on the fancy running stitch,
if God forbid it ever comes to pass.

Three years. She shows up unannounced.
The glossy ivory interlock's turned back
against a feather bolster against
a steamed-up window. *I called at nine.*
Listen to your bloody ansaphone.

The nightgown's a different matter.
Turn of the century, mangled lace
to the throat and cuffs. *Finest lawn*
she says, fingering the ankle length,
for a special occasion. Get it off now.

For the actual do – rummaging
the wardrobe – *he'll want... Yes,*
this black button-through
and the garter and stockings.

I'll Get Up Soon

I'll get up soon and leave this bed unmade

In the dream she sings it tuneless
but word perfect, a lyric she'd heard
only once and remembered:
the ballad of someone seriously out west,
alone but for a faithful dog or cat,
a creased apron discarded on a chair back,
a gramaphone gathering dust ... what comes next?

In the updraught of his breath,
a scent, *Rosemary I love,* Lapsang, liquid kippers
a weekend in a forgotten house *our honey*
honeymoon, she sings off-key, remembering
the disapproving registrar, the witnessed
tongue-tripped unsaid *plight thee my troth*
the knees-up later at his mother's flat,

his brothers dancing with his sisters,
the nephew with the tact and the zoom lens
just smile and give us the garter again
and all the glasses raised, proposing yet another
to the happy couple and may all your blessings
rest on the apple-pie bed, his mother's kiss
Goodnight, Mrs S. music all night through the wall

and how she took his fragile unknown face
into her hands, the new ring hard
and unfamiliar between her fingers,
wanting and unable to say anything
about the proper use of words and promises
and music and disharmony and these clean sheets
I'll get up soon and leave this bed

Years of descant and embarrassment.
My turn, he says, I'll make some tea for us
and pacify that bastard yodelling cat,
her dream voice echoing you've made your made your
made your song. Now learn to sing.

Romance

This is how he made her fall
in love with him. This is the tale
he always tells when he feels like talking.
The long one with the happy ending.

How he came by his sons, his daughters
our bold fathers, our pretty mothers
and the increasing shifting numbers of us.
This is where he finally won the prize

he wanted more than anything. She comes in,
her arms full, heading for the kitchen.
Awhile here, girl. I'm after telling them about
the night at Gallagher's I played the flute.

Now, surely to God, you remember that?
He winks to us, in no doubt. *I remember it –*
not breaking her long stride, smiling – *Indeed I do.*
And a terrible thing it was, if I may say so now.

He waits till she's gone. Remember this.
You never touch a Mayo tinker's bitch.
Nor any kind of laughing brazen
red-haired hard-of-hearing woman.

Vocation

A craving for coffee, for nicotine, for sleep;
　　　　　and a half world away
from Christchurch, from home, it turns into
　　　　　the corridor dream: the walnut parquet
of school, a random assembly of locked doors you pass
　　　　　and merely strum, hearing behind each one
the kept silence, a breathing presence,
　　　　　the static of a long distance call.

Your prayers you've learned to measure out between the bells,
　　　　　but it's the private litany
that troubles you, the things you recollect in poverty,
　　　　　rattled by the clipped accent
of beads, and sick of the sweet peculiar English scent.
　　　　　Old luxuries you turn in your pocket,
your nails snagged on the soft currency
　　　　　of warmed ivory towels, the barley white

and milk white fringes of a candlewick spread,
　　　　　a proper linen sheet; the coarse thread
of memory you finger, embossed white on white,
　　　　　the powdered imprint of your feet,
the pale impossibly expensive carpet of a cheap hotel,
　　　　　all life is sacramental.
Accost someone. Usher them into a sideroom, break the Rule,
　　　　　but make a deal, *let me speak,*

advise me and I'll pray for you tonight...
　　　　　Cruel, like offering chocolate
to a novice who owns nothing but her appetite,
　　　　　and futile when your own voice
might pursue you all day, echoing like a slap,
　　　　　an early morning call,
a vacancy that chills your back and will not stop.
　　　　　Barbara, my love, wake up...

*

Two years between the Holy Paracletes, the Carmelites,
            and you're advised to listen
and to wait. You've learned to still yourself, to sleep on trains,
            to abdicate decision.
Sometimes you falter, sidetracked between one order and another.
            You want to phone your mother,
who'll answer without faith *whatever makes you happy, Barbara.*
            You're no wiser than you were

at seven, out to celebrate the age of reason
            in a restaurant with your father,
Order what you really want. Ice-cream.
            And you chose vanilla, for the mystery,
the pleasure of an unknown name. When it came
            you swallowed disappointment,
spooned the ordinary white without a flicker,
            tempted to make much of it to spite him.

I think you have to reach your own epiphany, my dear.
            I will, you said. I bloody will.
You dodged the slap but it hurts you now,
            travelling through his territory;
the empty barely heated trains, greying sheep
            desperate enough to eat the ground
from under their own cloven feet. Whatever life there is
            the Yorkshire winter holds

suspended, dormant. You're cold but not without desire.
            You want snow. You want it now;
everything chastened, sumptuous, the pure simplicity
            of hidden country.
You want. You want. And what you get is Malton station
            on a mild mid-winter afternoon,
a waiting room, a slatted bench, a man who will not
            offer you a cigarette,

a steamy buffet door. Lean in on that door, discover
            that ice for the whole world
is delivered here. Sidestep the melting blocks,
            paddle to the counter,
tip up ten pence, ten New Zealand dollars, minutes after
            the banks have shut for Christmas
and wake stiff-necked, dry-mouthed with dreams
            just as the train pulls out.

Accept it now. The sky is not about to open for you.
You'll decide. You'll heft your bags
across the forecourt to a taxi and slide in.
Or you'll despatch them to the abbey
and turn away, unhurried, trusting as a woman
waking when she's good and ready
to a hand against her back, a voice, the combined incense
of a shared Silk Cut and coffee.